EVANGELISM 101

A Praxis / Practical Guide to Evangelism

ISBN-13: 979-8-9852078-0-4

Cover design by: Art Painter
Library of Congress Control Number: 2018675309
Printed in the United States of America

CONTENTS

FOREWORD

As a young first-grade student in the basement of my church's Sunday School building, our fabulous pianist Mrs. Baker related to me some simple but consequential truths. God loves me - I have sin which blocks my relationship with God - Jesus died for those sins - if I believe in Jesus and accept God's love, I can be a Child of God. Those truths changed my life. At that moment, I knew God wanted me to accept His love and in turn, to love Him. For Mrs. Baker's part, she simply made herself available, used her gifts, and trusted God for the results.

As a result of this event, and others along the way, twenty-five years ago, I started teaching Bible at a Christian school because I've seen the Holy Spirit change lives. It has been my privilege to be a part of God's work as He has made young men and women more like Christ. This process of discipleship begins with evangelism. Just before Jesus ascended into heaven, He commissioned His followers to, "Go therefore and make disciples of all nations, baptizing them in the name of the Father and of the Son and of the Holy Spirit, teaching them to observe all that I have commanded you. And behold, I am with you always, to the end of the age." (Matthew 28:19-20)

Although evangelism is essential to discipleship, it is often neglected. Sharing God's truth, hope, provision, and love to those who are not members of God's family is the call of every Child of God. However, because sharing the good news of Jesus requires transparently sharing ourselves, it can be intimidating. As we reveal ourselves to those with whom God places in our path, we know that the Holy Spirit comes alongside us and transforms people.

This book gives practical guidance to Christians who are ready to see lives changed, ready to grow as people, and ready to be used by God. When we as believers invest in evangelism and discipleship, we allow God to work through us for the flourishing of others. It was for this development of people that I was called to teach biblical truth to junior and senior high students.

One of the students my first year of teaching was Timothy Ross, one of the authors of this book. Together, with his family, his classmates, and God's blessings, we sharpened each other and matured towards sanctification in Christ. That process of becoming more like Jesus was only possible because others had invested in us with the Gospel. I am thankful this book guides all believers at all stages of growth to walk by faith in the area of evangelism. Increasing in our evangelistic skills, in our meditation of Scripture, and in our prayers for those around us, we become refined tools for the Holy Spirit to use for God's glory.

My prayer is that you find this book an encouragement and an asset as you join with Christ in the process of fulfilling the Great Commission.

In His love and service,

Scott Nandor
Principal
Talbot Graduate

INTRODUCTION

Welcome to Evangelism 101.

This is a piece in a series of projects that offer practical advice to the body of Christ covering a range of topics. This is not about theology or history, which are both important viewpoints that shed light on the topic. This project is about practical ways to approach a person, have a conversation, and possibly share the Gospel.

Not a great public speaker? Not a theologian? You are a great public speaker and a theologian? Keeping in mind the range from new Christian to a Mother of the Church, this project is written for a variety of perspectives. Some seminaries do not teach practical evangelism, as opposed to preaching, as it is either assumed or intuitive. So, it is okay if you have been to seminary or not, have multiple degrees or not; the person this book is for is the one who wants to better spread the Gospel.

Welcome to all those who want to join in God's work of spreading the Good News, of evangelism. You are in the right place.

GROUNDED IN SCRIPTURE

The Judeo-Christian Bible still has value in evangelism for us today. Yes! The past, some 2,000 years ago, has value on this topic today. Two goals can be accomplished by one task, reading the Bible can bring you closer to God and help you gain valuable tools for evangelism. People are people, and God is still God. People might not be walking long distances to wells anymore, but people want Living Water.(1) Evangelism is about hope; it is person to person; at the same time, a good foundation in the source document is a key to success. There needs to be a baseline to meet in order to then move into the practical side.

The Ingredients

This project is all about being practical. So, this section is to help focus the Christian on key areas we have identified to better evangelize for Jesus Christ. The parts, Knowledge of the Story – Seeing the Power of God... might be called something different in your church. Or, your church might include other sections in your theology. This project is not here to say that you are wrong but to simply provide a baseline for an evangelical conversation. Yes, we can have different theology and still be shining the light of God in the world together as we point to Jesus Christ.

Does learning the points described below stop the Holy Spirit from working the miracle of salvation? We believe learning theology, studying Christian practices and reading the Bible does not stop God's work but rather helps us get out of the way, allowing the person to hear God's truth as opposed to being turned away because we are ignorant of the Way.(2) This is similar to Christians saying they do not read the Bible because that would block the hope and love of salvation. We, as Christians, can do both. We can study the faith and walk in faith.

There are beautiful stories of unbelievers coming to believe in Jesus. There are amazing stories of visions or moments when they realized they are alive but should be dead. Those are God moments. It seems, though, that for the majority, they learn the story, something clicks for conviction, there is acknowledgement and some type of change occurs. These pieces do not have to happen in order. Some can take years to wander through each point and some can live a lifetime in a moment. For some, they will bounce from piece to piece again and again while others will move orderly from one to the next. One can even share an experience with another, yet no one will completely have the same experience as God is moving.

Each person is wonderfully unique, which means just as we should not put God in a box,(3) we should not put people in a box either. God wants to work in us for salvation, our own and others.

Knowledge of the Story

Most evangelism products focus on the knowledge of the story. For some Christians, the story starts in Genesis. For other Christians, the story starts in Jonah. For some Christians, it can only be found in the New Testament. No matter what, you need to know the story that you believe. You can keep your theology, but if you do not know how your journey connects to the Biblical story, it will be very difficult to engage with someone else.

In short, you need to know the information to make an informed decision. Reading the Bible is essential in this case. This is a vital spiritual practice. The Bible is limitless; there is always more to learn and read. But, your story, how it connects with Scripture and how it relates to someone else is a good baseline to speak from.(4)

Seeing the Power of God

How do you see God working in your life? This is Experience. There are many stories out there. You have a story – do not downplay God's relationship with you because it is not like Ananias, Philip or Stephen. Your story has power because it is God's story with you. If you degrade your own story, you degrade God's relationship with you and the godly work trying to be done through you.

So, how are you seeing the power of God in your life? Can you communicate it to someone else? Prayer / reflection / meditation is very helpful in this case. Also, it is useful to keep a diary or a devotional to record when something wonderful (crazy, unexplainable or an answer to prayer...) happens. There is a third piece to this, getting out in the world and being that answer to someone else's prayer. These are all great spiritual practices to help us see the power of God.

God can work wonders; God can and does work through you to be an answer to prayer. Often times, servant leadership / hospitality / standing up to injustice is the answer to someone's prayer if we are willing to stand. If you are not out in the world to do good, how is anyone going to notice God?(5) How is God going to answer your prayer if you are not working in the world? How powerful a witness can you be if you do not do good in the world?(6) How are you going to remember the wonders of God if you do not take a moment to thank God for the experience and to record it? This is what the Bible is, a recording of God's wonders.(7) In this case, you are continuing the story with your own faithful journey.

Conviction

This is what most people refer to as "the moment".(8) It is an awesome moment to experience. It is an amazing privilege to witness someone else's moment. But, it can take years to get there. It can take the help of many people along the way. Even in your own conviction moment, the Holy Spirit was there.

With that being said, no one can control it.(9) If you did not have complete control of your own moment, there is no way you are going to control the moment in someone else. This is not disappointing, this is liberating. It is not your fault if it does not happen. Rather, it is God's victory with that person and the faithful when it does happen.(10) You can be faithful by living out your spiritual journey with Jesus in prayer and trust in God to continue to work wonders.

Acceptance / Acknowledgement

But, there is another side to conviction, it is accepting the moment and responding.(11) This is Reason and Faith. Conviction can happen without acceptance, it is just like when someone realizes they have been caught but harden their heart.(12) This is another reason why it is a God moment, because we do not control their response.(13)

In a consumer / product-based society, many Christians get caught focusing on "how many have accepted Christ because of your testimony? I have ###". It is normal to want success and this is a great moment to look for. But, it does not happen alone. It is a moment outside of our control. And, AND, it is not final success. Their spirit is like a new born baby, and will need a place to flourish just like the Apostle Paul did.(14) They are a fresh sprout that needs protection (a loving community and a small group), water (encouragement), sunlight (insight and accountability), dirt (Bible and support), nourishment (discipleship and spiritual practices), and time to grow.

Some say "Acceptance", like Conviction, is a single moment while others say it can happen multiple times. Some say every time a person accepts the Truth about Jesus or does the good that God is calling them to do, they are accepting Jesus as Lord by living it out in their heart. There are plenty of good views out there. There are plenty of Christians who have different points of view but who are still helping others to become Christian.

So, what should we do in response to this moment? Pray! The Bible does not record an exact set of words we should pray, but we do know that there are examples in the Bible of conviction, prayer and baptism. There are plenty of resources that provide a model to pray. Some say there is an exact set of words to say to become saved. Some say that one must ask for the forgiveness of sins. Some say that one must reject all other gods in this moment. These are all excellent ideas. For the Gospel according to John, 20:30-31 simply wants the reader to know that Jesus is the Son of God and when we believe that, we have life in the name of Jesus.

We do not know your church, but we speak across the connection of Jesus' table. If your church points to Jesus as God Almighty, then the way your church does it is fine. Maybe your church could change a few things, what church is perfect? This book does not wish to stand in the way of your church's theology nor attempt to write everything about everything. There are great resources out there that can help you with prayer or more theology on salvation. This is a short guide covering a few basic principles to ensure a shared foundation in order to have conversation on practical ways to conduct evangelism. This short project is not intended to be an all-encompassing book on evangelism but just enough to spark the conversation that any Christian can be an evangelist.

Spiritual Sustainability

This one is a bit different than the other sections. The other sections are dealing with the spiritual movement from non-believer to a believer. This is looking at post-conversion. There are evangelism books that do not talk about the practical, which is where this book hopes to provide advice; most stop short, "Ya, you are saved!" THE END

Now what? There are plenty of spiritual practices, discipleship and other kinds of resources that deal with the post-conversion moment, just not from an evangelism perspective. We put forward the idea that post-conversion is also part of evangelism.

Jesus talked about the seeds that fall but do not grow (eaten by the birds), grow but have no base (rocks), grow without success (choked by weeds) and grow to produce more seeds.(15) Jesus points to the seeds that reproduce as a benefit to the world. From sowing to producing new fruit, each step is part of the whole process according to Jesus' analogy.

Now, there are theologians that argue about eternal salvation falling away, can someone lose their salvation… if there are no good works, how are they really saved… Good questions. But, the aim of this booklet is not to say that every Christian must do good work in order to be saved. Rather, our point is that every Christian, of every theology, agrees that there should be good works coming out of Christians; we will leave it to the theologians argue about how that relates to salvation in their own books.

If one looks through the Bible, the Testaments point to the Holy Ones of the faith, those who accepted God and did good works;(16) Noah had faith that produced good works that saved humanity; angels followed God's commands and Abraham's request to tell of the crisis and a way to salvation, saving Lot; Joseph had faith that produced good works, saving the future community of Israel; Moses was following God's commands and the community's prayers to speak of salvation and then produced good works to confirm the message; Jesus follows God's commands to spread the good news and confirm it with miracles; Peter and Paul follow God's commands to spread the good news and confirm it with miracles. Part of Deborah's, Elijah's, Huldah's, Jonah's, Jesus', Peter's, Paul's and others' message (Psalms, Proverbs, Isaiah…) is that they were to do good acts and to join a godly community along with repentance and acceptance.

So, encouraging people to join a Christian community is part of evangelism. Encouraging people to do loving acts in the name of Jesus is part of evangelism. Servant leadership, serving at a food bank or homeless shelter, small groups, spiritual practices and hospitality are part of evangelism.

This is not to say that encouraging fellowship and servant leadership are not also a part of discipleship or any other Christian subject area. Rather, it is to acknowledge that evangelism is more than selling fire insurance or a single moment. It is about teaching the story of God and hope through word and deed.(17) It is about showing the love of God through personal acts of service. It is about praying for the conviction of the Holy Spirit on souls. It is about witnessing the acceptance. It is about encouraging growth through fellowship, piety, discipleship and spiritual practices.

Misconceptions

One – It is not "a moment". The Apostle Saul / Paul did not have "a moment". Yes, there was the road to Damascus. But, there was the testimony of Jewish Christians, like Stephen,(18) that introduced Saul to the story of Jesus. Acts 9 is not the next day. There is a period of unknown time between Acts 7 and 9. Then, the "blinding light" appears in Acts 9. Saul is not converted then. Saul goes to a house and waits, without food and is in prayer, for 3 days. Finally, Ananias shows up. This means that there are at least four moments for the Apostle Paul. This is a journey of moments that has a mountain top moment (conversion) leading to more moments.

Two – We need to walk in faith. If Ananias was not willing, would you have been willing to take his place to help Saul become the Apostle Paul? Ananias is less famous than the Apostle Paul, but Ananias still had an amazing role in God's plan by walking in faith.

Ananias volunteered. This means that we need to pray and trust the Holy Spirit to place us in situations where we can work for God. This means we need to be willing to volunteer. It also requires that we be willing to be involved in the world so that we can be placed in situations where we can be the light. The situation might be a moment for us; but, in God's plan, it is helping the other person with their moment.

Three – We need to know our material. Trust and walking in faith do not negate knowledge of Scripture and church Tradition. One can say they are a Christian, but if one does not have spiritual practices (read the Bible, pray, corporate worship) … then, how strong is their faith?(19)

Jonah knows the facts of the message.(20) In Acts 8. Philip is moved by the Spirit to a location; Philip walks up to the caravan, notices something to talk about, and asks an honest question, "Do you get it?" The Ethiopian responds which Philip uses to continue conversation on what he knows. Like Stephen before in chapter 7 and Ananias in chapter 9, Philip teaches what he knows. Saul, the Apostle Paul, argues from what he knows in addition to having miracles worked through himself by the Holy Spirit.

It does not appear to be just facts but knowledge from their personal lives.(21) They have a conviction. They are not teaching facts about the mundane world but something that gets them moving. Stephen was only willing to die for more than facts, a meaningful true relationship with the Savior of the universe. After the teaching, the Ethiopian asks to be baptized. Philip baptizes the Ethiopian.(22) If we want to be used like Stephen, Philip, and Ananias, then we need to know our story in the greater Story as we walk in faith.

Four – We need to get involved in people's lives. Jesus got involved as he invited people into his ministry. After the healing of Saul (future Apostle Paul), Saul was baptized. In the text, it does not say who baptized Saul and it does not matter; however, it seems unlikely that Ananias was there to heal Paul but not participate in the baptism. The baptism happens after the healing. Saul connects with the disciples in Damascus. Shortly after that, Saul starts to preach.

This mirrors Philip's interaction in Acts 8. Philip is moved by the Spirit to a location; Philip walks up to the caravan and pays attention to what is happening around him. The Jewish Scripture is being read and so begins a conversation pertaining to what is happening. Ananias has insider information from God. The Ethiopian has a conversation with Philip, accepts salvation, sees a miracle and continues without Philip. The Ethiopian did not need a miracle but a conversation to believe.

If the disciples were not willing to go (volunteer and lead), the early Church would be a very lonely place. Churches were started based on the disciples willing to jump in, volunteer and lead. We can invite others into the spiritual practice of reading the Bible. We need to practice our own discipleship, be willing to have conversations and invite others to join us.

THEOLOGY

Theology, or the way one sees God, is important in this case. This project attempts to avoid theology, preferring to discuss praxis (practice) but it does acknowledge three points: God loves everyone. Everyone needs God. The Good News is for everyone.

One can see the ingredients (Knowledge, Power, Conviction, Acceptance, Sustainment) in the stories of the OT Prophets, Jonah, Jesus, Peter, Paul... We see this with Martin Luther, John Wesley, Martin Luther King Jr....

There are arguments as to when the Good News started. Did it start with Jesus or before? The Good News is that God loves us, an idea found in both the Old Testament and New Testament. The Good News is that humans can be saved from this world (Noah, Lot, Rahab, Daniel, Jesus, Revelation), which is an Old Testament and a New Testament idea. Jesus comes and personalizes it but it does not mean that the Jews were not loved any less or that the world is loved more. The Good News started when God promised in the Garden of Eden to save the world.(1)

This means that the promise is to all the descendants of Adam and Eve. Every person living today is a descendant of the first people, Adam and Eve. Before we were born, we had the promise of salvation which is fulfilled in Jesus Christ. This means that everyone can participate in it no matter who they are. This is the Good

News.

There are arguments as to whether or not the Good News can be shown or spoken. For this project, the idea is that the Good News is for everyone from a God who can relate to anyone. There are advantages to both methods. Some are really good with their hands (or at sports) and some are not. The message of God is not limited to those who can preach well or are so outgoing that they can talk to anyone. This means that the ways of communication are endless and since some communication is physical (offerings to the poor, servant leadership) then the Good News can be verbal or physical.

TIMES ARE CHANGING

THE CHRISTIAN WORLD NEEDS TO WAKE UP.

The world - Space exploration, retail, tech, world politics, schools, organizations, ect... IS CHANGING.

Yes, the housing market crashed. Yes, big companies that gave great pensions went under. The tech bubble came and went. A time where people could graduate and walk into a good paying job is over. This was in the 90s and 2000s. Now, we are in the 2020s and the world is still changing.(1) Traditional storefronts are struggling. Has the church adapted to the times?

K-Mart is gone.(2) Toys-r-us is gone.(3) Blockbuster is gone.(4) Polaroid is gone. Borders is gone. Tower Records is gone.(5) Nokia failed to innovate. Xerox failed to innovate. Yahoo failed to innovate. JCPenney failed to innovate. MySpace failed to innovate. Sears is failing. Macy's is failing. RadioShack is gone.(6) Papyrus, known for mailing cards, is gone. They have been around since the 1950s but who sends cards anymore?(7) America's drinking habits are changing.(8) Pier 1 is declaring bankruptcy.(9) It has been around since the 1960s.(10)

"In 2019, US retailers announced 9,302 store closings, a 59% jump from 2018 and the highest number since Coresight Research began tracking the data in 2012."(11)

"A record 9,500 stores went out of business in 2019, which seemed massive — but as many as 25,000 could shut down permanently in 2020, mostly in malls, says the an estimate from Coresight Research."(12)

Baseball is not the national pastime anymore.(13) More than that, sport's writers are talking about how if it does change in 2021, there won't be much of a professional sport at all.(14)

Television has faired no different. The 2021 Oscars showed this. The studio to win the most awards was Netflix verses businesses that have been in the industry for generations. (15) The ratings were down verses the 2020 and 2020 was worse than 2019 and 2019 was worse than 2018.

Notice the pattern? 2021 has not stopped things changing. If major industries, America's pastime, are changing and having to adapt, why not the church? There will be styles going out of fashion and new ways of doing things. The only constant is change itself. This has been the way of the world longer than the U.S.A. has been around.

What is the relationship between churches and the stores listed above? CHURCHES ARE TRADITIONAL STOREFRONTS. Think about it – storefront property, inventory to maintain (stain-glass windows still require upkeep, organ, pews), customers (members leaving in droves) and staff. It is no surprise, therefore, that they are struggling just like their non-religious counterparts. We need to recognize that the world around us is changing and if, like the businesses of yesterday who failed to adapt and innovate, which led to their death, we fail to adapt our conversations (16) or innovate practical ways to get the Gospel out into the world then we will die as well.

A Time of Transition VERSUS
God's Pruning

Refocusing the Faithful

This is a new time for the local church to succeed.(17) God's pruning is pushing us to be better. This is a time for leaders to look
at what is important. How can we more effectively reach people?
This is a time when churches are making hard decisions, cleaning
up finances, looking for money that was buried as well as looking at streamlining their policies and processes. There is no better
time to work for God.

Easy Access

There has never been a time where access to the Biblical Story is so
easy. One does not have to even buy a Bible anymore. Technology
has changed access for billions. There are also many commentar-
ies that explain much of the Bible. For the original story tellers, the
children of Abraham did not have easy access to the story. In the
times of Jesus and the early Jewish Church that spread the Gospel
to the world, access had not changed. It was really not until the
mid to late 1900s that the Bible became so accessible. Now a person can follow the sermon on their phone and the big screen, hear
it again on Monday, receive an encouraging word on Tuesday...
Our forefathers and foremothers dealt with the change, adapted
and successfully grew the church. Are we going to follow in their
footsteps or fail to adjust?

The Forgotten Tale

At the same time, the Biblical story itself is becoming more and more unknown. Again, looking back across history, the children of Abraham were being taught their story. This was a "two birds one stone" situation where their story was intertwined in God's story. As time marched on, the children of Abraham became a nation-state, then a kingdom, then an exiled nation. But, their story was still interwoven in God's story of redemption. As Jesus came and later Peter and Paul, the story was expanded to non-Jews. Now, 2000 years later, the expansion is around the globe with people with all kinds of family lines.

On one hand, the expansion allows a Christ follower to be from anywhere. Christianity is not locked on one location. There are believers around the world. You can go online right now and find a beautiful sermon from Kenya, a scholar from Lebanon, a preacher from Mongolia, a minister from Tonga... The technology that is filling people's lives is an opportunity to connect more and more around the world.

On the other hand, the church has struggled to adjust to the situation. Some are afraid of this as they see churches dying. For this project, "dying" is simply God's pruning which was predicted. We can all agree there are areas in our churches that we want to improve. Pruning is not scary as it is intended for new growth. God has been preparing the Church. What new opportunities await the Body of Believers!!!

This is the opportunity that the local church has today. The knowledge needs to be more personal (local) and meaningful (someone needs to teach it). With God's help, we can shine in the darkness. Let us not be afraid of hope. Let us see the past blessings of God as a way to move forward and shine with our own faith to the next generation.

SOCIAL SKILLS

The preceding sections form a baseline theory to work out in the real world. Only so much can be done in the library or classroom. We are going from theory to praxis. Just like the disciples before us, we have to get out into the world. We can be the hands, feet and month for Jesus to help save humanity. Again, this project realizes that changing dynamics means that the church needs to adjust. There is nothing written on a practical approach to evangelism? Let's write one and help the church be God's witness to the world.

So, with the above in mind, let us jump into the practical side of evangelism. There are two main parts and a third part for church leadership. One side is the social side, social skills. The other side is weaving the Gospel into the social. These are distinct; one can be social and not Christian, or social and Christian and not spread the Gospel. Also, one can be a Christian and try to spread the Gospel but the social skills are lacking. The majority of this project is focused on both of those issues. There is a third part, advice to leadership.

In all of this, it is okay to read ahead. It is okay to focus on areas you feel best connect with your skillsets. It is okay to try something to see if it can be a new skillset that works for you. It is okay to read the leadership section even if you are not a leader. This project is hoping to encourage all Christians to step into faith and be a tool for Jesus Christ.

Improving Social Skills

Below are a break-down of three social skill levels to help the reader become more confident in approaching strangers to start creating a connection and to be able to show the love of God to them. In "Communicating the Story", there is more focused advice on the Gospel itself. In this section, "Social Skills" is focused to just approaching people in general. This is about building confidence in social settings so that, when one gets to "Communicating the Story", we can have the social skills to make connections for the Gospel. These could be used in a business setting. So, little steps will lead to big steps. The plan is trying to move from knowledge into action. This means practice. And, with God's help – we can be the light to the world.

Soft Skills

Soft skills are interpersonal skills that are useful in just about every human context. To not mention them would be unfair to the reader while to include them would take away from the advice concerning conversations and make this project longer. Plus, some of the soft skills can be problematic during a pandemic (shaking hands, proper way to sit across from someone while eating…). So, if one is unsure as to whether or not they need to work on their soft skills then this project encourages all of us to ask their church family and friends for feedback. Also, the internet has many resources on this topic. Soft skills are not Christian or non-Christian, they are social skills for everyone and can change depending on the situation, location and culture.(1)

Skill Level Novice – The Brute
(Anti-Social to Shy)

For some, you are the type that find approaching people difficult or have felt unworthy to be approachable. So, let's work on that together.

Knowledge

For this project, evangelism is for everyone as everyone needs the Good News. For you and I, using a sport's analogy, the Good News is that God wants you on the team. The playing field is not just heaven but God wants us to play on Earth, too. Jesus came down to spread the gospel, and the salvation changed people's lives on Earth. God wants us to make a difference in people's lives for eternity, in this life and the next.

So, remember, the Good News is for everyone, so it is for you. To help reinforce that, a devotional over the Psalms with the Gospel of Mark might be really helpful for you. A Psalm a day (if you miss a day, that is okay. No fire from heaven will come down, just keep trying)(2) and a chapter of Mark a day (so two chapters in all) is a great way to get started. If we have a good (not perfect, but good) understanding that God loves us, it will outflow to others. No one is perfect, not David or Peter. Yet, God still wants to love us.

Also, evangelism is not necessarily about preaching on a box in the middle of the street. It can be a neighbor talking with their neighbor. It can be acts of piety or servant leadership that people notice and ask you, "Why do you do that?" Not everyone is good at speaking, that is okay. Let's jump into the rest of the project to work on getting better together.

Prayer

Also, for this project, just as evangelism is for anyone so is prayer. When is the last time you prayed for yourself? Sometimes, we forget to pray for ourselves as we pray for others. Praying to be useful to God is not selfish. Praying "God, help me to better understand your will..." is a great prayer.

Acts 13:3 is where Barnabas and Saul (who later is referred to as Apostle Paul) have the church lay hands on them. Laying on hands is a way of blessing. They are being blessed to do God's work. Self-care, reflection, meditation and praying for yourself is okay. The Psalms are full of personal requests and this kind of discipleship.

The other side to this is, do we believe in our prayer when we pray for ourselves? If you pray to show God's love more, do you believe that you are loved? Lastly, do we put higher expectations on our prayers towards ourselves as opposed to praying for others? God's timing is different for everyone, are you okay with a delayed response for your friend but not for you? Also, do we give more grace to others but not ourselves?

If you are a child of God, then you are loved by the God of the universe. If you realize you are not a child of God, then God is still there loving you. You are always welcome to join the family. A short prayer is below, or pray with your pastor.

"God, thank you for your love for me. I want to live for you. You died for me so that I could be free. Please be with me always. Amen."

Mental Exercises

"Do unto others as you would have done to yourself..."(3) One of the best ways to do this is to practice self-love. What is self-love in the Christian sense? If you do not listen to God about yourself, how are you going to hear God's will to be there for others? If you cannot forgive yourself, if you cannot believe that God forgives you even though you accepted Christ, how is God going to use you to forgive others? If you cannot laugh at yourself and acknowledge your mistakes while knowing that God still loves you, how are you going to share your faith journey? A healthy self-love is understanding your identity in Jesus Christ, you are a child of God.

Forgive yourself when you are not as friendly as you feel you can or should be. Self-doubt and self-criticism are crippling. It is okay to be nervous. It is okay to remember the past with shame. But, when the past becomes an obstacle to living in the present, that can hurt your ability to move forward. Forgive yourself.

Acknowledge who you are. It is okay to laugh at yourself as others laugh at something funny around you. Are they laughing at something funny that happened or are they making fun of you? People who are funny are being laughed at. Comedians want people to laugh at or with them. The difference is difficult to define between someone being mean when they laugh and someone laughing at a funny moment. It is okay to laugh.

Roleplay (the Christian term would be "meditate") in your mind and in front of the mirror. "I am loved by God." "I am worth being loved because God loves me." "God wants my prayers." "God knows my name."

Social Exercises

Say "Hi"

There are people in the world today who HAVE TO "talk" to you. No, not family or neighbors. These are cashiers and baggers at grocery stories. These are the people who drop off mail or pick up the trash. These can also be those working in sales or marketing. And, chances are, you will have an opportunity to "talk" with them. Now, by "talk" this is not a really long conversation or even a 5-paragraph essay. Let's start with something simple, let's just say "hi".

You are in front of these workers for a few minutes, it is completely fine if you say "hi" to them. Besides, they probably already said "hi" to you. They are taught to say "hi", so it is okay to be taught to say "hi", too. You might have already told them that you do not want any bags. See, you are talking already and you did not even notice it. This is how easy it is to make a connection. Since you have the light inside you, you are well on your way to sharing Jesus with the world.

Keep working on just saying "hi" back to people who say "hi" to you. This is a conversation in today's world. This is the start on your way to be more social.

More Than "Hello"

Now, "hello" can be an easy trap. A classic complaint of communication and relationships is that they are shallow. So, as a Christian, we should try to show compassion by trying to get past "hi" or "hello". It is okay to try something in the environment you are in. It might be awkward at first, that is okay. It is like walking, we don't remember – but we all tripped and fell as a baby and as a kid.

Another typical problem of humanity is that we do a really good job of casting judgement. So, try a compliment to open the conversation. The compliment is not a question. The only response might be a smile and this is okay. This is a safe way to create space to grow conversations.

If you see a kid going crazy, talk to the adult, "wow, I love your example of patience…"

If you are standing in line and you notice a product that you were going to buy in the shopper's basket in front of you, ask about it.

Or, if they have the same shoes (purse, hat), "Ah, great minds must think alike…" This is more of a joke but it can be used to break the ice and talk for a moment.

SKILL LEVEL APPRENTICE – AVERAGE

You are preparing for the next step, Advanced. Yes, we can get there. Even the people involved in this project series are not all advanced. We are all at different levels. This is okay. The levels are subjective as well. Also, you can read ahead. In short, this project is for all of us trying to make a difference for God.

Knowledge

This is Scripture and Tradition. Whether you have been studying Scripture and the Holy Ones (Saints) for years or just started the Christian walk, it is okay to focus on certain themes as you prepare to evangelize. Scholars study for 50 years and do not know everything.(1) This is a positive sign; it means that there is no expectation for us to know everything. It would be a good idea to read another resource outside of this project to get some more theological perspectives. One way to do this is to ask your pastor for their suggestions. For this series, there are books that have been reviewed. Also, a web search may be helpful.

Prayer

This is walking in Faith. This does not change from the last section. Jesus needed prayer, how much more for people like us? The book of Psalms is a great text for meditation.

Mental Exercises

This is Reason, Experience and Faith. It is the same as above, Golden rule, forgive yourself, laugh at yourself.

Roleplay in your mind and in front of the mirror. "God loves me..." (There are many great resources out there that talk about this – you are loved wholly and completely by God. And, from this project's perspective, the more you feel and understand that, the more it will pour out to others. This love is unique to Christianity and a great resource in evangelism.)

As you get more comfortable, try roleplaying with a church family member, friend or peer. It is okay to ask your pastor if there are others who want to evangelize as they might be able to connect you with them. You could be a small group.

Also, realize that you are worth having a conversation with. You are a child of God, and you are worth God's love. If you have never read through the Psalms or the Song of Songs, now might be the right time. Psalms deals with a lot of self-doubt. Song of Songs is a healthy look at personal image and interpersonal relationships.

Social Exercises

Yes, this is the same activity as above. But, some situations are similar and some are different. The more situations you are in, the more practice you have, the more confident you can become. So, keep talking to strangers in line at a store. Mix it up. Try to make sure you are not just talking to one type of person. The easiest way is to find a connection, but it can also make habits. We are looking to be flexible. God loves everyone, so we need to be willing to talk to anyone.

SKILL LEVEL JOURNEYMAN – ABOVE AVERAGE

As with all of this, it is okay to read ahead. It is okay to look back. Trust God and walk in your interests, passions, and be willing to get out into the world.(1) Some days will encourage you that you are growing. Some days will make you question everything. This is okay; questions are okay; we are human. Stay in connection with the body of Christ, keep reading the Bible, pray, and walk with God.

Knowledge

It is okay to learn about communication techniques, love languages, different personalities or marketing techniques. There is nothing wrong with using science to better one's self. It is great to learn another language. It is awesome to learn Bible verses and study theology.(2)

But, remember to trust. The "trust" does not mean we do not learn.(3) We need to learn and get educated about the Scripture even if it is not with a certificate. We need to know the Biblical story. We need to know our story and how the Biblical story relates to us. At the same time, there is a lesson of balancing facts and trust. The Apostle Paul was told no.(4) Philip listened. They were successful because they trusted the Holy Spirit to be at the right place at the right time. Facts with God directing the steps is going to be walking with the Holy Spirit.

Prayer

The focus in the beginning (Beginner level) was self-care. Sometimes, with any book or project, one can get overwhelmed with too much information. This point, praying for others, is just as important whether one is a beginner or an expert.

Mental Exercises

Just because one gets to the top does not mean they can forget the basics and what got them there. You will still have good and bad days. This is a part of life. Notice, learn, adjust, grow.

Social Exercises

Keep trying to stretch yourself. It is okay to try. Just because you are at the next level doesn't mean there won't be any surprises. Walk in faith.

Talking to people outside the store...

I am walking into the store with my two boys, there is an older couple finishing up putting their items from their cart into their car. I approach, "Can we take your cart? My mom always..."

This starts a two-minute conversation about values, old times, parenting...

Something catches your eye –

There was a guy walking with this bright, colorful fish bag (think of a tropical fish but the size of a laptop bag). I was walking by and I complimented him on the bag and asked if it was a laptop case. We had about a two-minute conversation.

Doing your chores –

At the gas station, I was pumping some gas. A car drives up, music blaring on the other side. Guy gets out, starts pumping gas on the other side of the station I am at. So, there is about 10 feet between us. I can see a bit of him as he is standing there. I ask, "Hey, what song was that?" He responds, "It is from … Something released after he died…" We talk for about a minute. I am saying, "Cool… Cool…" Conversation ends. As he is leaving, he calls out, "Hey man, you have a good day." I respond, "Hey, thanks. You too." Music starts blaring again as he drives away.

COMMUNICATING THE STORY

What is the Good News? It is God's love to others and to you. This simple message means it can be communicated in many ways.

You need to know your own story. You need to be able to fit it into the Biblical narrative. You need to be able to show, by words and / or deeds, this story to others.

"A high degree of imagination is required of those who trust in God." Douglas John Hall

It is the Christmas story, so caroling is an option for evangelism.

It is Jesus' life, so intro Bible Studies are a good evangelical option.

It is Jesus' death, so a class on wills, trusts, and retirement are also a good evangelical option.(1)

It is Jesus' practice of prayer, so prayer groups are a good evangelical option.

Jesus was concerned for the burdened, so volunteering at a home-less shelter, half-way house, food bank... are all good ways of showing the evangelic message of Jesus.(2)

Giving the Story

"In the second chapter of the Acts of the Apostles we have the first sermon preached in the power of the outpoured Spirit, which is a perfect pattern for true Christian homiletics to the end of time. It is from first to last an appeal to the men (and women) who were listening. Peter was not preaching in front of the people and won-dering whether they would like it. He was preaching to them. And the difference between the preaching that does nothing and the preaching that does something is the difference between preach-ing before people, and preaching to people."(3)

Peter was preaching because of wonder. People were asking about the possible miracle happening before them. Peter's sermon was great for his time points to remember, is in that setting. But, for many, Christian and non-Christian, they do not know the story. So, preaching the way Peter did might not be the best method for each setting you find yourself in, Paul did not necessarily replicate this style. But, Peter is, in the moment, answering the question be-fore him. This is something that we should pay attention to – give the Gospel to those who ask.(4)

Over-Doing It

Yes, we can over-sell. This is an issue with trust. Are you the one-person team who feels like they have to do it all because everyone else on your team is not as good as you? In ministry, in evangelism, do you realize that you are on God's team and if you are trying to do everything, are you pushing God out of the moment? Over-Doing it is all about the lack of trust in God's plan for the other person.

You can be that pushy salesperson, the desperate guy / gal who is trying for that date, or the "comes over too often neighbor". Most of us know a story or two about this, and it is a fuzzy line to find. But, try to find a good balance (Golden Rule) and avoid overdoing it. It is okay to let the conversation go. If it feels like you are pushing it, you probably are. If they are not responding, then are you dictating the conversation? You are not God, and God gives everyone a choice. If you are taking the choice away by forcing the Gospel, are you anti-God? You cannot control the situation nor the conversation. Remember, do not put God in a box, controlling how the person should be saved. Also, could this be the only time that they will hear the Good News? Maybe. But, is everyone dying after you talk to them? No? Then, do not limit God's wonders and third member of the Trinity.(5) If you think you overdoing it, are you trusting God enough?

Trust

This does dip into theology, but the power of God is still working in the world today. As with prayer, one needs to trust in God's plan. This means our involvement while simultaneously working as a team and not being a "ball-hog" or consuming the conversation. If you are talking all the time, when the other person says "yes", is it their words or someone else's? Christianity is a team sport, and God is willing to play any position to save the world. Are you willing to let God play? Or, do we not trust God enough to win souls?

Prayer

With that said, prayer is key. It is a major theme in this project. If Jesus prayed, we need to pray. Pray for yourself. Pray for others. Pray. Now, most of us do a pretty good job for praying for others. In our move to be unselfish, some Christians forget to forget to pray for their own self. Christians are really good to pray for their sins, the church, and world peace but often forget to pray for faith, for greater love, and the right words to say in every moment. It is okay to love yourself and pray over yourself. Pastors, before they preach, pray for themselves ALL THE TIME.

"May the words of my mouth and the meditation of our hearts be acceptable in your sight, O Lord."

"May the words that I say be Your words and not my words, O Lord, our Rock and our Redeemer..."

If you want to be used by God to introduce Jesus, it is okay to pray for yourself. It is okay to pray for the Holy Spirit to use you. Church leaders do this, and who says you are not a leader? Who says you cannot pray for yourself? Even Jesus prayed for strength, are you better than Jesus? You are a sibling of the Most High, of Jesus Christ, and you need to pray.

Relevant

Active listening is important. Reaction is important. If they, seemingly randomly / out of the blue / without prompting / no prior conversation, say something spiritual, "I think hell is stupid..." "This whole end of the world thing..." "My mom used to go to church. I don't..." Think "God moment", step up to the door that God just opened and walk in. That is the metaphor which means, CONTINUE THE CONVERSATION. The Holy Spirit is working, are you ready to help? Are you willing to be Ananias?

Making the Point

Ever notice who comes to the door? Who stops your walk down the sidewalk? Some topics are acceptable in certain settings. What advertisements are around? The places or activities can help clarify the point you are trying to make. If you talk about the importance of obedience to God, but are breaking the local regulations, this will hurt your point. Think about what comes to mind at certain places... Speak to your audience.

Caroling

This is one of the few times of the year that people are willing to listen to Jesus music. "Hark the Harold Angels Sing" and "Joy to the World" are excellent classics. This is a fun time where anyone can be invited to a church event, even non-Christians. The carolers do not even have to go to strangers' homes, but to the home centered (homebound, shut-ins). This builds community, creates a fun space to ask questions and presents an opportunity to share the Gospel. So, it is okay to invite non-Christians to the event. It is okay to ask around the church neighborhood if they would like some carolers to drop by. Encourage members to ask their neighbors if they want some carolers to show up.

Church Events

A lot of churches host community outreach events. This is a great way of helping outsiders feel comfortable with church. Remember, people have all kinds of experiences with church and this means that some have terrible experiences (child abuse, racism, gossip...). Yet, even though churches host these events, people showing up to your church service is not guaranteed. Evangelism can be intentional and in church events, should be intentional.

When organizing a Church event as a tool or an avenue for evangelism there are some questions church leaders need to ask themselves before proceeding with any planning or organizing a committee. The planning committee should start with these three questions before deciding any event: Purpose, Placement, People.

Purpose: What is the main purpose for the church event? Is it outreach, hospitality, or is it truly for Evangelism? If the purpose of having a church event is for Evangelism, then what is the theology, tradition, and culture of Evangelism that the church has agreed on? Will the Evangelistic event be done by Word or will it be a musical event with an altar call component? Whatever the decision is, the first thing a committee has to know and come to agreement on is, "Purpose - _____.

Placement: Although the physical church facility has been the historical location for all church events. We live in a culture where the facility has become more of a façade of Christianity. While the older generations are reluctant to have anything new come into the building, the younger generations are reluctant to step foot on the campus. Therefore, does an Evangelistic event need to be on Church property? Or are we creative enough to bring the Church to where the people are. This is an equally important question because it influences who is willing to show up. If you want burnt out Christians to show up, are they going to come to something that is really overt?

"Placement - _____.

People: this is a crucial element to any evangelistic initiative. Is the event for the PEOPLE or is it just marketing the church? If evangelism is not all about getting the message of faith, hope, and love to the people that really need it, any church event is in vain.

Some churches host their own events and some churches set up a booth at a fair or festival. An important idea to keep in the forefront of our planning process is asking the question, are you forcing what you want to do on the planners of the event or asking to offer help? Does your church ask "what do you need or want?" or "how can we support you?"(6) On the other side, does your church create ideas without input from the community? One is providing a resource that the community wants and the other is putting in energy to a project that someone might want.

Holidays

As with caroling, there are a few events during the year that people are more open to talk about spiritual ideas or come together for an event. It may be Ash Wednesday. It can be Easter. It can be Christmas. Other less obvious holidays are Memorial Day and Veterans Day. This gets people thinking about death, so the reality and finitude of our existence becomes even more real if only for a moment. Also, knowing other holidays or major events that are not the mainstream allows for conversations. In Australia, there are Super Bowl parties. In the U.S., there are places that celebrate Chinese New Year. When the Olympics and World Cup happen, millions are tuned in. In Australia, Canada, and the British Isles, there are celebrations for the monarchy. These moments can create opportunities for conversations and connections.

Homes

Do car sales people drop by homes? No, for the most part, the sales are about homeowners' insurance, windows, house cleaning... This makes sense as the sales pitch is specific to the area. There are churches, businesses and organizations known for going house to house. Yet, is it effective?(7) The internet is becoming the best (cheapest, most convenient) way to reach people in their very homes without the awkward cold call moments.

With that said, neighbors can reach out to neighbors. If there is a crisis, it is okay to ask, "Would you like to talk to someone? My church has a Care Team... My church has a pastoral team..." This is asking the person if they need some spiritual care / pastoral care and some evangelism. Remember, evangelism is the whole spectrum of hospitality to conversion to discipleship to theology to spiritual practices.(8)

Library

This is a great place, like the coffee shop, to pull out a Bible and study. If the library allows study groups for students on math, physics... what about having a Bible study on the Psalms? You can be kicked out if people are offended, so be mindful of the topics. There are plenty of topics that are non-offensive and point to Jesus - a theme like love, hope, spiritual practices or wisdom / Proverbs. Hospitality will be more important here than proving the point.

Movie Theaters

This is a great place where people are:

Probably all there for the same thing (standing in line waiting for the movie)

Don't have a lot of options to distract themselves. (as they stand in line)

You can be the distraction.(9) You can ask about Jesus, but that might be too direct. Asking about their spiritual background could be a good start. Or, if your pastor preached on something that is possibly relevant to the people standing next to you,

"Hey, I was at church, our pastor mentioned universal Truth (or responsibility to care for Creation; the Golden Rule; forgiveness...). I am still wrestling with this idea, what do you think?"

The point is not to win. The point is to introduce yourself and an idea. The fact that you question / doubt but still go to church is difficult for some to understand but for those on the outside of church who are questioning, this can be a point they can relate to.

Notice that you say "wrestling" as opposed to doubting? You can believe in something but still not have all of the answers.

You are surveying the audience. The audience is the person / group next to you. What do they think? By saying that you are trying to figure it out means that you are open to possibilities which helps them relate to you and, hopefully, be open with you by continuing the conversation.

Park

Oftentimes there are channels where a lot of people walk through and parks can be one of those spaces. Kids can hang there and be safe. Have you ever thought about having a guitar playing and people just hanging out? Creating a music space, is great because it happens throughout Europe, the Americas and Australia. Yet, you are not looking for money but rather a holy conversation.

The Call Back

This is so critical. If someone gives their contact information, they are literally saying, "Yes, I know you are going to reach out. I am okay with this." People today know that giving a cell phone number invites a call. Are you taking advantage of that? If your church hosts an event, people do not have to give their contact information. So, the ones who do? Call them. Remember, evangelism is also about sustainment / discipleship / relationship / small groups. It is not about a single moment.

Tracks

Tracks and pamphlets are a great resource. A business card, pens, and even little stress balls are excellent resources that bring the idea to hand. With so many ideas (ads) that are just visual, it is nice to have something that breaks the mold. This is why calling back (or even a text) is so important.

But, how does one give an item safety with all of the health concerns going around? Many churches stopped giving out items which was and is considerate. There are pro's and con's to either choice.

The best advice we can give is to be consistent with the decisions on tracks and meeting together. Also, there is no need to argue over this resource. For those who do not feel comfortable, let them abstain and honor their decision. For those who do feel comfortable, let them proceed and honor their decision. Churches have fought over enough. There can be more than one right way. Support the decision of the leadership.

Self-Care / Sustainment

Now, there are books that teach and teach about all kinds of facts. This book does something similar but with a warning from Ecclesiastes. Do not worry about learning everything. Teachers and authors give the impression you can know everything but that is just not possible. How does this one book capture everything about the subject? Can a person read every book ever written, even the books that have not been written yet and the ones that are yet to be found by historians and archeologists? Just not possible right? Or, can a person know what is in the heart of every living person, all at the same moment? No, that is overwhelming right?

Does one know everything about every spiritual practice? Lastly, just to drive home the point, can a person know where each star is in the sky or where every animal is walking? No, that is silly right? The same is true with knowledge. We, humans, need to be realistic about knowledge. It is okay not to know everything. It is okay to be curious and learn something new. It is okay to ask questions. It is okay to learn a new spiritual practice.

So, this project is not designed so that the reader can learn and remember every word. This project is hoping to be big enough for each reader to come away with something. You can be like a worker (business, medicine, law...), a jack of all trades or specialize in a sub-field. So, pick what resonates with you and excel at it / them. If some advice does not fit, it might just not be for you. Some are not salespeople but they are great at preaching. Some are great at computers and art but they really love singing. We cannot be everywhere and do everything just like we cannot know everything.

So, please do not try to learn and be an expert on every point. Rather, find what works for you and hone that skill (work on improving it). In other words, you do not have to be an expert on the Trinity, grace, free will and the End Times. It is okay to be really knowledgeable on grace and have a basic understanding of the others to begin with. Or, be an expert on church history and an intro level on theology. The local church needs all kinds of workers working on their craft. The world, and God, is big enough that we need all kinds of talents (skillsets).

Also, know your own story. Don't distract yourself with facts so much that you lose yourself. Write an autobiography. Keep a journal. It is not a point of pride but bragging on God's promises as you record the blessings, miracles and moments where you saw God coming through for you and you can share that as a reason for your belief in God.(10) The Apostle Paul did this all the time. (11) Your story is a great asset to evangelism. There are plenty of people out there with someone else's facts but there are not a lot of people with someone else's facts (the Bible) and their own story (I believe in prayer because I prayed and my prayer was answered...). Some grownup (our mom's and dad's or others) probably told you that the world is round, that 2+2=4, and other good facts that are true. But, it is when you can see it for yourself that it becomes your own story. This is how Jesus taught differently in Mark 1:21-28.

Novice

In working up the skill to talk about the Good News, depending on your situation, you might want to skip certain people. For example, if your uncle hates Christianity, you do not have to start with him. Continue to pray for him and look for opportunities with other people. Remember, "novice" means beginner even if this means you are looking for someone inside your own church. (12) Also, just because they say something does not mean you have to respond right away. Their words might just be God's door to the next conversation.

Look for conversation starters (look back at social skills for insight). Then, look for opportunities that they bring up in the conversation that can be linked to the subject (i.e. – hope, love...) that you are trying to bring up. Some people have been burned by Jesus lovers or Bible thumpers (people who literally hit the Bible as they shout condemnation on the audience or people who really hit others with the Bible). You do not have to talk about Jesus or the Bible. What does the person bring up?(13) The idea is to start the conversation, start the relationship and introduce Jesus or the Bible along the way. These are just examples to help you think about linking Biblical / Christian themes to everyday conversation.

Parents died? Listening can be the best action you can do. Psychologists and psychiatrists, police, leaders, and pastors are given classes on just listening. Businesses value listening skills. Listening is an action. If they ask, there are possible connections to love... The hope of eternal life...

Sports? This could be connected to a church league. Can this be connected with fair play? Right and Wrong? Maybe you know of a Christian on a team that you could talk about?

Burdens at work? Listen to their worries and concerns. Jesus did not just talk all of the time, Jesus listened. If they ask, this be connected to self-care, meditation, prayer, the Sabbath...

Struggle of work / life balance? Listen. Can this be connected to prayer, meditation, self-care, the Golden Rule, the Sabbath?

Relational problems? Listen. Can this be connected to prayer, the Golden Rule, Proverbs?

Politics? Can this be connected to right and wrong? Golden Rule? Tithing?

Fears about the economy? Listen. Can this be connected to hope? Church's work in the community?

Cancer? Pandemic? Listen. Listening shows you care. Can this be connected to a visit from the church? Hope? Prayer? The meaning of life?

Final exams? Can this be connected to Proverbs and discipline? Stress and hope? Many just need a friendly person to vent to; this can be a great opportunity to be silent.

Holidays? Can this be connected to the meaning of life?

Riots? Listen. Can this be connected to the evilness of humanity?

A listening ear is a great witness.

Race topics? Listen. The Church can be honest about the past with both the positive and negative. The Church is full of stories of Christians at the front of these issues, pushing for justice. The Church is also full of stories that are painful and heart wrenching. The Church is also full of Christians who used their power in negative ways and forgiveness needs to be asked for the past and current actions of the Church. One way to approach this sensitive subject is through listening and honesty. There are a lot of hurting people so listening and honesty will be refreshing to any conversation even if there are those who disagree.

APPRENTICE

Now, depending on your situation, again, you might want to skip certain people. Family can be scary. Friends can be scary, too. Start with church members and get comfortable there. As you get more comfortable with your story, try with more people. Evangelism is not always Jesus, Jesus, Jesus. Sometimes it is the blood drive at church or a video game night with the youth.

Again, just because they say something does not mean you have to respond right away. Listening can be the best activity in a situation. Listening is an activity and good listening can be really hard to do. It can be the next conversation where you bring up what they mentioned in the last conversation. For many in sales or negotiating, getting the second conversation is a goal. It is okay to pray on it. Don't beat yourself up over hindsight. Use your insight learned in hindsight for your next conversation.

Look for conversation starters (look back at social skills). Then, look for opportunities that they bring up in the conversation that can be linked to the subject that you are trying to bring up. At the same time, try introducing topics and see where the conversation goes. Christians should not manipulate the interactions but create opportunities for relationships. Relationships can grow into invitations to church, maybe a Bible Study or even a relationship with Jesus or be turned down entirely and that is okay. Some people have been burned by the Church, so do not try to manipulate or trick for Jesus. If they are interested, they will continue the conversation. Like the Apostle Paul, getting invited back is a sign you are doing something that connects with the other person. You do not have to talk about Jesus or the Bible. What are they talking about? The below are just examples, like the examples for the novice, to help you think about how Biblical / Christian themes relate to everyday conversation. There might not be anything different from above other than the conversations might be deeper and more complicated than the ones above.

Parents died? Just listen. Sometimes the best action one can do is to sit in silence. Then, as one prays and meditates on the situation, maybe connect the conversation to biblical topics. Can this be connected to love? The hope of eternal life? The hole inside everyone? Heaven? Maybe the church is hosting a class on grieving that could be helpful.

Sports? Can this be connected with fair play? Golden Rule? Rules in general? Maybe you know of a Christian on a team that you could talk about?

Burdens at work? Listening is a useful activity as well. Can this be connected to what we are really here for? Purpose? Adam and Eve?

Struggle of work / life balance? Can this be connected to Purpose? Cain and Abel? ...

Relational problems? Can this be connected to Abraham? Isaac and his sons? Maybe a small group at church that could help? (maybe help start a small group?)

Politics? Can this be connected to right and wrong? Golden Rule? Leadership? Broken world?

Fears about the economy? Listening is a good option. Can this be connected to hope? Eternal life? ...

Cancer? Disease? Pandemic? Hand Washing?

Final exams? Can this be connected to expectations...? Stress management / Prayer / Meditation? Maybe invite them to the youth group?

Holidays? Can this be connected to purpose...? History of the Church (Good and bad)? Hope? Sabbath?

Gen X and Z to the Baby Boomers are all different. No group of people are 100% like another, because age, location (local, national and international), work, education, family, culture interests, religion, etc. all play a part. Back to "Don't put God in a box"; do not lump people into one group. Their insights, feelings and interactions can be as varied as the colors in a rainbow. It does not mean there will not be overlap; who likes to be in a quarantine? So, walk in faith and use the knowledge and growing experience you have to engage with others.

Journeyman

Again, just like with the social skills, this is not teaching the experienced something they already know but rather tools to help pull the apprentice up to the next level. At some point, you will realize that you can notice the person, learn a little about them (this can take hours, days or weeks), and either by listening or by dropping connecting comments you can bring up biblical and Christian truths which can lead to deeper conversations about God, life, death and the plan of salvation.

Please do not lose the fact that we are not selling a product but sharing love. People have been really hurt by religion, by Christians, and / or the local church. There are ways to manipulate conversations but that is not pure and holy. There are fire and brimstone ways (think OT prophets and Paul) and compassionate ways (think Abraham and Jesus). Don't judge other styles and it is okay to try different ways but try to stay true to your values. If you don't believe in hell, you probably shouldn't use a fire and brimstone style; if you believe in honest and truth, manipulation is only going to push you away from your own faith.

Calling

In a quick survey of the authors of the various "mini's",(1) no one likes to receive cold calls. Now, cold calling does work. But, there does not seem to be any hard evidence on how well cold calls work whether it is over the phone or at the door.(2)

However, calling to continue the connection? This works. Please call back. No, they did not call but if they say they are interested, then they are literally saying, "Hey, I am interested in hearing about the Gospel..." CALL THEM. Ask about them. Listen to them. Connect with them. Talk with them.

Teams

No matter if you work by yourself or with another person, please remind yourself that you are still working as a team. You should still be walking with the Holy Spirit. There is value to go by yourself. There are examples in the Biblical text that show this.(3) But, Jesus encourages pairs over individuals. There are dangers to working in a group or as an individual. Teamwork / infighting, set your own schedule / lack of mutual support, these are just a few positives and negatives for each one. Brainstorm (meditate) and pray over this. Talk with mentors and your pastor. Sometimes, the example needs to be shown and one must go alone. At the same time, there is probably someone willing to go with you if you ask. There is safety in numbers.(4)

LEADERSHIP

Manage your team – The local church is a franchise for the bigger universal Church. The local church is the traditional storefront. This means that there needs to be people working in hospitality and advertising. Now, this is not a traditional sell where we sell peace and joy to the highest bidder nor is hospitality only given to a certain class or background. Rather, we need people willing to announce the love and grace that Jesus Christ offers to all nations.

Leaders need to think creatively about creating ministry pipelines (volunteer opportunities) in their church that can become mentorship opportunities that allow people to grow into greater responsibilities. The story of the talents... Little jobs can grow into big jobs... Small opportunities can grow into greater leadership opportunities. There are hospitality teams. There are evangelism teams. There are Bible studies and youth groups. Everyone wants the funny person on their team. Everyone wants the one who speaks two languages on their team. How can the leadership create ways of collaboration, teamwork while guarding from over-stretching and burn-out?

Is there a member who talks all the time? Is there a member who would be considered a social butterfly? One can silence them. But, they probably would be a good fit for an evangelism group.

Is there that one person who loves meeting new people? They

could be a good fit greeting people at the door. Or, they could be a great fit at a welcome table where greeters bring new people. Or, they could be on an outreach team. This allows for flexibility of personnel as all of those jobs are a part of evangelism. It also presumes that one has enough staff to have multiple teams or stations.

Some people like to be involved with everything. Some people like bouncing around from place to place. Some people love to multi-task. So, maybe move that person every 6 months so they do not get bored, they can have a variety of experiences and lend their growing expertise to each group as they rotate.

Maximize the Team

As a leader, please try to notice your teammates' skills and utilize them. You should know your people. The individual might not have the vocation of sales but might be a great people person. Some local churches focus on hospitality over evangelism. Some local churches try to do both equally. There are many ways to work this out in your local setting. It is okay to try one method for a period of time (try a year as anything else is usually too short to create confidence in the practice and see results) and adjust as necessary.

Not everyone has to be in the job of "evangelism". Some like to be behind the scenes. Some like administration or counting the offerings. People can have overlapping skillsets. Now, one can argue that there are many ways to evangelize, and this project would agree that working on stage (giving an altar call), the front door (welcoming people), parking lot (greeting first time visitors) or behind the scenes (working on the website) can all be excellent ways to get God's message out, but sometimes terms scare people.

So, as a leader, adjust. How does their skillset or vocation best fit in the church? Do you want to win a debate over terminology or simply encourage people to volunteer in the place that fits their skillset the best? Not perfectly, but the best for the current culture / direction of the church? In the nursery (protecting the future generation of leaders while the current generation of leaders can focus on worship, Bible Study, small groups...)? Co-leading a Bible Study? Behind the scenes setting up the tech?

Mentorship Opportunities

Social media is huge and it is only getting bigger.(1) Maybe this is a good way to get a shy person comfortable talking with strangers about God through a non-personal medium.

Passing out bulletins can turn into passing out flyers... Can artwork become graphics for the online sermon?

Walking down an aisle to light a candle can grow into reading the Scripture on stage or through an internet platform; it can lead into speaking about Jesus on the street or calling members of the church to be active again.

Watch out for ageism,(2) racism and other biases. These issues are going to be anywhere there are humans. On one hand, there are those on the outside that look at Christianity as the "white man's" religion. There is some historical truth to this false claim, how are you going to acknowledge and work through this? On the other hand, many look through a colored lens even though almost everyone knows that appearances can be deceiving. But, it is the reality we live in. It is encouraged to acknowledge, talk about these issues and ensure everyone understands and carries out God's practice of love and forgiveness.

Certain People

People are not a place. However, most people know their place, where they are supposed to be and where they are not supposed to go. It is said all the time to people from youth to retired folk, "You are a leader..." But, when they come with an idea? They get patted on the back and told, "That is so nice, thank you." Yet, more often than not, the pat becomes a soft guide out the door and they are not allowed at the table or even in the room.(3) This happens to minorities – those dealing with racism, sexism, ageism, or other forms of bias.

Please recognize; PLEASE! They are a set of experts. They are a target audience. Anyone can be a minority in church due to the different power dynamics inside and outside of church.(4) If we push our own members out the door –

Who will be left?

Why would they want to invite (evangelize) their friends and neighbors?

Why would they evangelize for the Boss (God) while middle management (you) pushed them out?

As a leader, you are not paid to lose. If leaders, looking at evangelism, push out the unwanted (youth, old, ect...) then you are the coach limiting the players who will want to play for you. Jesus did not do that. Jesus picked blue collar, educated, youth, married, single, retired... And, for evangelism, God is calling everyone to be on the team.

The Youth

The youth, teenagers and pre-teens, are a great resource. College students will be in the work-force in just a few years, the church needs them now. Every church wants them but so many treat them like the worst sort of minority.

They might not know the traditions, but they also might not have the habits that might inhibit creative thinking. Yes, they might not know the history, but their perspective is gold. Their insight can be better than any consultant because it can be instantaneous (as opposed to calling in a consultant, review the situation, discuss… when the resource is right there, just ask them) or because they have grown up in the church. They might know the culture of the church better than the pastor. No opinion is gospel, but they are God's children just like you are.

You are a leader now. They can be leaders now. Christians brag that Jesus was able to take the uneducated and start a worldwide church. Jesus has that accomplishment. As a leader, can you brag? The Apostle Peter and the Apostle Paul could brag about what was done through them. Is the lack of diversity limiting God's plan?

The youth can help advise the church on what they know best. They can help advise messaging to the youth, working with social media, possible best practices for using video in the worship service, etc. Have problems getting the youth to accept Christ? They might be the best evangelists to kids, youth, young adults, young families… Hospitality needs them. ("Hey, spouse, did you see that kid? She was so helpful. I want our kids to be like her." "Ya, they are giving her a position in the church; almost like an internship. That is going to make her more competitive for college and job placement. This would be a great place for our kids to grow up.")

Everyone in Between

For the authors, there has been discrimination against religion, (5) place of origin,(6) and even been accused of theft.(7) The discrimination mentioned was just the list of the discrimination that was experienced for just one of the Euro-males. There is discrimination. If one denies it? To deny discrimination is to deny that it can be done at all. An injustice anywhere is a threat to justice everywhere.(8) Discrimination can happen anywhere to anyone at any time.(9)

What does this have to do with evangelism? Every person has blind spots; issues that they cannot see. By being inclusive, one has a better chance of making fewer mistakes as well as making hospitality, love and grace more universal. It is not watered-down theology but enhanced community with accountability of the members themselves and a wider array of skills.

The church needs input from men and dads.(10) The church needs the input of women and moms. The church needs those who do not fit into those categories – youth, single, veteran, sports enthusiast...(11) What church doesn't want dads? Not just men, but married men with children. But, what about the single guys? Churches want youth, but Boomers? Churches want minorities, but what about international students that do not fit the category?

Diversity

They are needed You are needed as you have insight that can help the church. Your personality, preferences, connections, hobbies and skillsets are exactly what is needed to connect with people to help them know the story of the Gospel in a personal way. You are that person.

We connect this way as veterans who are perfect strangers, "Hey, you were in the Navy? I was in the Navy..." We connect this way over sports when sitting at a ball game. Moms connect with other moms; Dads with dads; grandparents with grandparents; random fans that start talking at concerts; hikers on a trailhead; we find something similar and we connect.

This is all part of the culture of the group. It can take time to connect, so the more diverse the culture of the group (sports and tech and sewing and cancer recovery groups and music and, and, and). Also, there are different titles that one can connect to, race, gender, interests or where we are from.

Clichés

These points of connection can create clichés, so be careful. However, this idea of connection is not just cultural but Biblical. Peter connected with fellow Jews. Philip connected with a fellow scholar. There were adjustments and growing pains, but they pushed to be inclusive to Mary mother of Jesus, Saul called Paul, and to those who received the out-pouring of the Holy Spirit. This is how the church has grown. People can connect to the culture they can relate to. The more points of connection the group can make to the new individual, the stronger the relationship can be and the more members can connect with the new individual.

Retired

Retired people? They are a great resource. They were just in the workforce, so who is better to tell best practices than those who were just there? They are the missionaries who just returned from the field, having personal experiences in the workforce to tell the next generation. The church still needs them now. And, just like anyone else, new pastors to ministry or tried and true pastors new to the church, there might need to be some adjustment (the church calls it grace, the business world calls it orientation). They might have some habits that clash with the church functions; they do not need to run the church, but they can run a program. Again, they might not know the history, but who knows every facet of church history?

They know their history. They have their own culture. But, they might know the culture of the church better than the last few pastors that were there for a few years apiece, whereas they could have been in the church for 50 years. Their insight into the relationships at church is faster, more precise and deeper than any internet search. They have lived what the youth are studying today. They have led through crisis, disasters, and ate with sinners.(12) They are the parents of the church. Their insight is gold. They might be best suited to manage the hospitality team or a Care Team.

Hard Questions

If you, as a leader, realize that your church is not growing, one must ask:

"Who am I pushing out?"

"Who am I not empowering?"

"What is stopping members to connect with their friends about Jesus? Me?"

"Do people really feel loved here?"

Hospitality

Hospitality inside can be evangelism on the outside. But, speaking of hospitality on the inside of the church, traditional storefronts, like restaurants, use the 10-5 rule. Companies try to create a culture of hospitality, so it is something the church can learn from. (77)(13) If you are within ten feet of a guest, make eye contact and acknowledge them. If you are within five feet, say something. Being acknowledged while entering shows that the organization is paying attention. Being acknowledged while leaving shows that the organization is caring.

If the person looks confused or lost, it is okay to say,

"Welcome, I am Mary. I am on the hospitality team learning how to help people. Do you need any help today?"

"Welcome, I am Jordan. I am on staff here. We are here to help and answer any questions. You look lost..."

This allows the other person to see that we, the church, are okay to ask questions because everyone is learning. Everyone is new at some point. Trying to be welcoming is a great first step to evangelism.

The W's

Who are you looking for? (the mission)

A church is open for anyone but it is difficult to focus on everyone. The result could be that you are stretching too thin to be of benefit to anyone. By knowing your target audience, your organization can look for ways to serve / reach the community.

What about your organization is going to attract your "who"? (self-reflection)

What is your organization doing with music, speakers, social media...?

Where are the people (the "who") you are looking for? (location)

Look for activities that match your target audience. For a quarantine, calling people is a great way because everyone is home. Try to maximize the use of technology.

Why are you attracting those "who"? (the reason)

This is where your theology fits in... This is where the nursery fits in. This is where the culture of the church fits in. So, what is the culture of your church? It could be mono-culture(Boomers only, no kids; a white or black only church) But, is it welcoming? Is it discerning (a Christian way of saying questioning)?

How are you going to attract the "who"? (action)

Prayer is vital. Walking in the Spirit is critical. Role play, brainstorm and encouragement are all key. Spread love to the members inside. Then, you have to get onto the field and play. Call a member and share a joke. Call a neighbor and ask for some prayer. Go through the church directory and practice showing love. The word will get out. If people feel loved, they will invite others.

STOP TELLING PEOPLE TO BE JESUS

We need to stop telling people to do what Jesus does. People showed up for miracles from Jesus. Who is doing miracles of feeding 5,000 at your church? Can you imagine your intern acting like Jesus for pastoral care? It would be a disaster. Should your Care Team start walking into hospitals and touching people like Jesus did?

Why do we do the same for evangelism?

We are supposed to be like Jesus, spread the Gospel, love others, pray... We are supposed to have Fruit of the Spirit.

As leaders, it is our responsibility to train those under us. If the Bible is useful for "teaching ... and training in righteousness", are we, as leaders, teaching / training or just giving a nice catch-phrase? When we say, "Be Jesus", we are trying to tell them to love as Jesus did and that is good. But, when Jesus was asked how to pray, Jesus gave specific advice. "Be Jesus" is so broad that we lose focus and it is not good leadership. In the saying, "be Jesus", we are often neglecting mentorship opportunities and the moment when we should be giving practical advice – soft skills, prayer, honesty, be yourself, listen to the Holy Spirit... Have the conversation with details. Read some books. Try something new. Be a leader like Jesus.

CONCLUSION

We hope that this book inspires you to be the light of the world and be salty.(1)

In short, know your story and how it relates to the Bible, walk with Jesus, be personal and try. That is not all evangelism is, but you have a good starting point. You are not alone, you have the Holy Spirit. Talk with your pastor. Pray and meditate. Listen to what the other person is saying. The times are changing, but God is still doing wonders. Jump on God's team and get out there, digitally or in a safe physical way. God is playing right now; we are doing this together; come join us in the ministry to the world. Thanks for reading Evangelism 101, and God bless.

101 – BIOGRAPHIES

Juan Lara is a 1st generation Mexican- American who grew up in Los Angeles, CA. While in college, he was in the leadership team for Intervarsity Christian Fellowship at Pasadena City College. He had the opportunity to go on mission trips to Turkey. He also attended School of Ministry at Expression 58, a church in Glendale, CA. Juan's work experience has been in sales, working two World Series in food sales, and currently sells life insurance.

Mateo Lavea Mamea is a member of the United Methodist Church. He has a degree in Human Communications from Cal State University Fullerton, and currently is pursuing a Master of Divinity degree from the Claremont School of Theology. Mateo and his wife Nidia enjoy spending time together watching old scary movies, reading, reflecting and living in gratitude in Southern California.

Monica Mitri is a member of the Coptic Orthodox Christian Church where she's been a Sunday School teacher since 2006. She has a Master of Theological Studies from Claremont School of Theology, and previous degrees in business and literature. Monica currently lives in California with her husband Michael, engrossed in reading her theological books and drinking coffee.

Paul Park is a 2nd generation, Korean American, that grew up as a pastor's kid in Koreatown, Los Angeles. Trying to run away from God, Paul Encountered the Grace is God during his period of rebellion. Paul received his calling into Vocational ministry and is passionate about multicultural/multiethnic/multilingual ministry. Paul is currently preparing to launch a new church in the city of Westminster, CA in 2021 called Free Life Community Church.

Ryan Cullumber will graduate from Claremont School of Theology with a Master's of Divinity in Spring 2021. Ryan also has a dual undergraduate degree from the University of Pittsburgh in Business and History. He is a member of the Disciples of Christ in Southern California. Ryan is married to Sadie, a Disciples pastor, and has two girls Willow and Indigo. Ryan has been very involved in the overseas ministries of the Disciples through his time serving on the board of Global Ministries. He is focused on building community wherever he is called to serve after graduation.

Timothy Ross has a degree in Biblical Studies from Azusa Pacific University. A United Methodist; U.S. Navy combat veteran who deployed with the U.S. Marines in Afghanistan and Europe; his latest jobs were the U.S. Embassy in Australia to assist during the G20, teaching Chaplains and Chaplain Assistants; and working a World Series game in food services. He is a part-time pastor. Tim and Nadia currently live in So-Cal with their two boys.

Timoteo Young grew up as a 4th generation Pastor's Kid (PK) in Wilmington, CA. His undergraduate was a Bachelors of Divinity at Kanana Fou Theological Seminary in American Samoa. He is working towards a Masters of Theological Studies from Claremont Theological School. As an ordained Pastor, he works as the Regional Youth Director of the Southern California Congregational Christian Churches. Timoteo and his wife Stella and their 5 kids reside in Norwalk, CA.

EDITORIAL NOTES AND SOURCES

Thank you to Josh Thomson, John Freese and Chris Johnson for their proofreading the text.

Thank you to Jackie Tisthammer, Campus Scripture Specialist working in the InterVarsity North Bay Area, for feedback on best practices of evangelism.

Also, the format used did not support endnotes nor footnotes. So, the list below was used to help track the sources. This might not be the same for future pieces of the project.

Introduction

None

Grounded In Scripture

(1) John 7

(2) Acts 18:25

(3) Richard Peace, Holy Conversation: Talking about God in Every-day Life, (2006, InterVarsity Press,) Pg. 38.

(4) 2 Timothy 3:14-17

(5) Matthew 5:14

(6) James 2:14-16

(7) John 20:30-31

(8) Acts 2:37

(9) Acts 10

(10)   Numbers 11:27

(11)   Acts 2:37-42

(12)   Esau, Eli, King Ahab and Queen Jezebel would be good examples

(13)   Luke 17:11-19

(14)   Acts 9:19

(15)   Matthew 13:1-23, Mark 4:1-20, Luke 8:4-15

(16)   Hebrews 11

(17)   Word only without deed is like being a hypocrite. Deed

only without words needs a partner who can explain.

(18)   Acts 7

(19)   Philippians 4:8-9

(20)   Book of Jonah found in the Old Testament

(21)   2 Timothy 3:14-17

(22)   And this is the connection to the Ethiopian Christians who have traditions older than the traditions in Europe or the Americas.

Theology

(1) Genesis 3:15

Times Are Changing

(1) This was written in January 2020, before COVID-19.

(2) https://www.forbes.com/sites/michaellisicky/2020/05/09/kmartdown-to-its-last-34-storesfinds-itself-to-be-essential-once-again/#3be5788c429c

(3) https://www.history.com/news/toys-r-us-closing-legacy

(4) https://www.forbes.com/2010/05/18/blockbuster-netflix-coinstar-markets-bankruptcy-coinstar_slide.html#3d6d7ef25464

(5) https://www.collectivecampus.io/blog/10-companies-that-were-too-slow-to-respond-to-change

(6) https://valuer.ai/blog/50-examples-of-corporations-that-failed-to-innovate-and-missed-their-chance/

(7) https://www.cnn.com/2020/01/24/business/papyrus-stationary-bankruptcy/index.html

(8) https://www.cnn.com/2020/01/14/business/alcohol-consumption-iwsr-report/index.html

(9) https://www.cnn.com/2020/02/17/business/pier-one-bankruptcy/index.html

(10)   https://www.pier1.com/pr_history.html

(11)   https://www.cnn.com/2020/02/17/business/pier-one-bankruptcy/index.html

(12)   https://moneywise.com/a/chains-closing-the-most-stores-in-2020

(13)   https://sportsworld.nbcsports.com/baseball-is-not-dying/

(14)   https://www.si.com/mlb/2021/03/17/baseball-preview-pace-of-play-crisis

(15)   Sarah Whitten, "Academy Awards ratings plummet to all-time low as viewership drops below 10 million", Apri 26, 2021, https://www.cnbc.com/2021/04/26/oscars-2021-academy-award-ratings-plummet-to-all-time-low-.html

(16)   This does not mean change the Bible or change our theology but it can mean utilizing technology and changing our vocabulary so that those hearing can understand.

(17)   https://www.youtube.com/watch?v=JxhmcXTUSGo;

Saddleback Church led by Pastor Rick Warren in California. In the first few minutes, Pastor Rick talks about how Saddleback Church helped 24,404 people come to Christ in 2020. That was a record for Saddleback.

Social Skills

(1) This project was written for the English speaking world – Australia, Samoa, Hawaii, Canada to England. Just as there are accents, there are differences in the soft skills / interpersonal skills between the countries and inside the countries (The U.S.A. has the South, Southern California, the Mid-West, New England (which is not a state but is the upper northeast states)) and also co-cultures (i.e. - First Nations in Canada...).

(2) Prayer and reading the Bible are spiritual practices. This means one needs to practice to be good at it. It is not like breathing where it comes naturally. So, you might not get it right the first few times. It might take years. But, that is the challenge and the reward for those who press on.

(3) Matthew 7:12

Skill Level Apprentice - Average

(1) Ecclesiastes 12:12

Skill Level Journeyman - Above Average

(1) This does not just mean physically, but it can be through a phone call or social media

(2) 1 Timothy 4:8

(3) There are those who believe that one does not have to read the

Bible, but just have faith and the knowledge will come.

(4) Acts 16:6

Communicating the Story

(1) If you have kids, it is highly recommended to have a will.

(2) There might be rules on what you can or cannot say. If you do not agree with the rules, volunteer somewhere else.

(3) G. Campbell Morgan, "Evangelism" (2016)

(4) Matthew 7:7-8; would it be any surprise if God does it to us and through us as children of God?

(5) There are arguments whether or not God still does miracles. We believe that miracles are happening today but we are not trying to push this belief. This is why this project uses the word "wonders". It can mean two ideas; as miracle as well as mean the natural wonders in the world overseen by God. The context of this project, wonders are attributed to God, how one wants to use theology beyond the point in this project is up to the reader.

(6) https://www.youtube.com/watch?v=uLHwOsNLWKY

(7) https://digitalcommons.liberty.edu/cgi/viewcontent.cgi?article=1232&context=doctoral

(8) A family started attending not because they did not know Christianity, church, and Jesus. It is because they did not know hospitality from a church family. They had been burned by church not because of sin but because church was not welcoming.

(9) Please keep in mind soft skills and guidance during a pandemic or even just the flu season.

(10)   Joshua 4:1-9

(11)   Philippians is a great example of this.

(12)   During the pandemic, the authors wanted to ensure that project also took into account the guidance and restrictions. The authors followed the guidance about social distancing and washing hands. But, the practices of self-care (washing one's own hands) and social distancing (Golden Rule; taking care of others) are not in conflict with this project's focus about conversations and building relationships. These practices were still able to be done through letters, phone calls and social media. In one church, a Care Team (just a group similar to a prayer team but is tasked with also calling members for basic pastoral care) was working with these ideas in mind. The membership did not shrink, the active members grew and finances are positive. This is during a time when many churches are hurting and people are still walking away from the local church. In another church, they postponed their start date but are still moving forward building relationships. For at least two churches, this project works.

(13)   Acts 17:16-34

Apprentice

(1) The whole project is focusing on practical advice for Evangelism 101, Pastor 101, Counseling 101, Church 101 and possible others. These are mini-projects in the bigger project of trying to give practical advice to the body of Christ.

(2) https://www.resourcefulselling.com/cold-calling-statistics/ ; https://www.prainc.com/tips-for-cold-calling-surveys/

(3) Jonah or Philip in Acts 8; both the Apostle Peter and Paul were

willing to work by himself or with a group.

(4) Safety is accountability, protection against accusations and personal safety. We need to watch out for each other so that we do not stumble into sin, get caught up in sin or accused of sin.

Leadership

(1) https://www.si.com/nfl/2020/11/06/nfl-generation-z-fans-social-instagram

(2) https://theunstuckgroup.com/2016/05/3-reasons-your-church-may-not-be-ready-for-baby-boomers/; https://www.christianpost.com/news/are-baby-boomers-returning-to-church.html

(3) Matthew 19:13-14

(4) While this piece in the series is more tailored to an audience in the U.S.A. and the references and additional information is from situations in the U.S.A., the overall series was designed for Christians living in predominately English-speaking countries – American Samoa, Australia, Canada, England, Ireland, Scotland and the U.S.A. Research was conducted with this focus in mind and some of the surveys and references are not from the U.S.A. At the same time, the authors are either from or have lived in different places for multiple seasons which colors their worldview. This means that this project acknowledges the complexities of international bias, racism and privilege as well as the systematic racism in the U.S., colonialism, the repercussions of Trans-Atlantic Slave Trade.

Those born in the U.S.A., might have privilege compared to their cousins in their parent's homeland but also might have to deal with racism in the country their parents immigrated to.

Those who immigrated to the U.S.A., might have to deal with the hardships of adjusting to a new way of life, the lack of privilege simply because their experiences are not the majority's, and, at the same time, possible hostility from the one's back home who could not immigrate as well, and even their own privilege (more or less) due to how their country viewed their position (gender, religion, chosen profession…)

Third, there are stories where (many youth or retired) have been pushed out of the church. So, an all-white church ostracized the youth. Or, an all-Korean church… This book is about evangelism and is written for all churches. This creates an interesting perspective to try to balance.

With all of that said, how does age-ism work in that? Where in the pecking order within minorities? Is youth verses black? Or woman verses man? White woman verses a Hispanic man? Black or Asian? First Nations? Ph.D verses blue collar? How fathers are treated in church? Race relations are at the front of everyone's mind (2020) but just three years ago it was immigration. All of these issues are found in the church as the church has humans in it. Leaders can take these problems to be worked through or as the church helps take a stand.

In the end, this project is trying to stay focused on evangelism and even though there are overlapping subjects (theology, Christology, eschatology, Trinitarian, public speaking, personal communication…) we have mostly skipped those very important subjects. Yet, for diversity, we do not wish to say that it is more important than salvation, but we wish to acknowledge the church's past with sorrow (Jesus, and our church family, please forgive us) and a sense of pride (Jesus, thank you to those who pressed against the glass ceilings, the barriers to education, restaurants, pools… and for all those who helped make the church in Your image). This is an important issue that can help impower the church to greater communion or bind it to stagnation and forfeit its call to the kingdom of God.

(5) blue collar – David, James and John; educated – Philip; youth – Samuel, John the Baptist; married – Moses, Peter; single – John the Baptist; retired – Elisha, Matthew retired from tax collecting the moment he walked away.

(6)   2 Corinthians 7:13-15

(7) Denied a higher paying position because the individual was a Christian. This happened in the U.S.A.

(8) Denied access to services because, "We don't have to... You are an American." This happened in the U.S.A.

(9) It was ageism; "young kid..."

(10)   Martin Luther King, Jr.

(11)   This does not get into privilege, power structures, "what is racism?" or "is everyone a racist?" Great topics for discussion, but as with other topics (i.e. - assurance of salvation, trinity...), they have been left out simply to focus on the subject at hand.

(12)   Sitting in a North Carolina Baptist church in 2008, the pastor comes up, "Today is Father's Day. Now, we are going to do Father's Day a little different this year. I am new, but I heard last year, for Father's Day, the church passed out a book on how to be a better father. Well, we are not doing that again. I apologize for that. When Mother's Day or Father's Day shows up, you are going to get a flower. Next year, we might do something different. But, for now, last year is not repeating."

(13)   Dads can love sports or not be into sports. Moms can be a veteran. There are all kinds of categories that can unite or divide. The authors said it in a particular way to spark curiosity so that

the reader could think about other categories and challenge possible mis-conceptions.

(13)   Psalm 145:4-7

(14)   Knowledge outside of the church is not always a threat. Good business practices are not a threat to the church's finances. Better ways of using social media are not a threat to the Bible.

Conclusion

(1) Matt 5:13-16

www.ingramcontent.com/pod-product-compliance
Lightning Source LLC
Chambersburg PA
CBHW071928020426
42331CB00010B/2763